Boundaries

Boundaries

Are You Boundaryless?

Oliver JR Cooper

Also By Oliver JR Cooper

A Dialogue With The Heart – Part One: A Collection Of Poems And Dialogues From The Heart

Trapped Emotions – How Are They Affecting Your Life?

Childhood – Is Your Childhood Sabotaging Your Life?

A Dialogue With The Heart – Part Two: A Collection Of Poems And Dialogues From The Heart

Toxic Shame – Is It Defining Your Life?

Abandonment – Is The Fear Of Abandonment Controlling Your Life?

Child Abuse – Were You Abused As A Child?

A Dialogue With The Spirit - A Collection Of Poems And Dialogues To Help You Grieve The Loss Of A Loved One

Trapped Grief - Is Trapped Grief Sabotaging Your Life

Note to Readers

That which is contained within this book is based upon my own experiences, research and views up until the point of publication. It is not to be taken as the truth or the only viable viewpoint. It is not intended to diagnose or cure any disease.

This book is dedicated to Simon Rose. Thank you for showing me what it means to have boundaries and to be assertive.

Boundaries – Are You Boundaryless?

Edited By – Jessica Coleman

© 2016 Oliver JR Cooper

ISBN-13: 978-1535324748
ISBN-10: 1535324740

For information, please contact:

www.oliverjrcooper.co.uk

Contents

Introduction...1

Chapter 1: Anger – Do You Have Anger Problems? 7

Chapter 2: Anxiety – Do You Suffer From Anxiety? ...11

Chapter 3: Approval – Do You Worry About What
Other People Think?.. 15

Chapter 4: Empathy – Do You Experience Too
Much Empathy?.. 19

Chapter 5: Intimacy – Do You Find it Hard To
Experience Intimacy?...23

Chapter 6: Isolation – Do You Isolate Yourself?.........29

Chapter 7: People Pleasing – Do You Have The
Need To Please others? 33

Chapter 8: Receiving – Do You Find it Hard To
Receive?.. 39

Chapter 9: Relationships – Do You Lose Yourself
In A Relationship?...43

Chapter 10: Saying No – Do You Find It Hard To
Say No?... 47

Chapter 11:Sense of Self – Do You Lose Yourself
Around Others? 51

Chapter 12: Skin – Do You Have Skin Problems? 57

Chapter 13: True-Self – Do You Find it Hard To Express Your True-Self? 63

Chapter 14: Ungrounded – Do You Find it Hard To Stay In Your Body?...67

Chapter 15: Walked Over – Do People Walk All Over You? 73

Chapter 16: Walls – Have You Built A Wall Around Yourself?..79

Chapter 17: Weight – Are You Overweight? 83

Chapter 18: Developing Boundaries 89

Acknowledgements 97

Introduction

When someone gets to the age when they are old enough to go to school, there is a strong chance that they will be in a class with people around the same age as them. When starting primary school, they are likely to be around six years old.

By this age, they will have reached a certain level of development. Now, this is not to say that they will be the same height as everyone in their class or even have the same level of intelligence, but they should be able to cope with the work that is provided.

They may have the same level of intelligence as most people in the room, or they might be in a position where they are slightly above or below the others. However, it will only be a matter of years before they leave primary school and go up to secondary school.

Once they reach this point, their appearance will have changed dramatically. Also, one could find that they are now roughly in the same position when it comes to how they match up to others, at least in terms of their level of intelligence.

What is also likely to come into greater focus during this time is the kind of relationships they form with their fellow pupils (or 'students'). They could be seen as someone who is outgoing and confident, or they might be seen as being the complete opposite.

How they are perceived by others could match up with how they were perceived at their previous school, or it may be that they have changed since then. At this age, they might be happy with how they behave, but on the other hand, their behaviour could be something that causes them to experience pain.

1

Based on their level of development, they are unlikely to believe that they can do anything about what is taking place – it could be seen as just being how they are, and that's the end of it.

However, if they are happy with their behaviour and the kinds of responses it creates, there is going to be no reason for them to get worked up. Along with this, they could also experience relationships with others that are extremely rewarding.

After a number of years have passed, their time in mainstream education will come to an end, though they could end up going to college or university, for instance, where their experiences could be the same. This could be a time when they can continue to enjoy their life, or it could bring them yet more pain and heartache.

These are not the only experiences that can occur, however, as their life could be fine one moment and then it could end up changing. In this case, something will happen, and their behaviour – along with their relationships – could change.

This can then cause them to feel as though they have no control over their life, and this will be an experience that some people are only too familiar with. If this were to take place, it would allow them to realise what it is like for people who have always experienced life in this way.

And, when someone feels as though they have no control over their life, they can end up experiencing all kinds of challenges – from finding it hard to express themselves, to saying no, to having the need to please others, and suffering from anxiety, amongst other things.

One way of looking at this would be to say that regardless of how long one has had these challenges – or any others, for that matter – it could be because they haven't developed any boundaries. And as they haven't developed a strong sense of themselves, this causes them to suffer unnecessarily.

On one level, boundaries allow someone to say yes and no, as well as knowing where they begin and end, and where others begin and end. On another level, boundaries will allow them to feel safe in their own body. Therefore, having boundaries allows someone to feel safe physically as well as energetically.

The reason why this can be something that has affected someone for their whole life is because boundaries are usually formed during their childhood years. So, if this was something that didn't take place, it is to be expected that they will have suffered in one way or another for all these years.

During these years, there is the chance that they experienced some kind of abuse or trauma, and this is then why they don't feel safe in their own body. If someone has experienced abuse, it doesn't necessarily mean that they were physically abused, as the term could relate to another kind of abuse.

Perhaps their personal space was not respected during their childhood years, and this then stopped them from being able to develop boundaries. They would then have remained boundaryless, and other people would be seen as a threat to their survival on a deeper level.

On the other hand, if this is something that has occurred after a number of years have passed, it could be a sign that an external experience triggered something within them. Perhaps there were certain parts of their life that weren't right, but this was overshadowed by the parts that *were* right.

These parts counterbalanced the parts that caused them pain, and they may also have become accustomed to them. It then became normal, and the only thing they knew.

Due to everything that has been triggered, these people are in a similar position to someone who has always experienced life in this way. Either way, what this shows is just how important boundaries are.

The trouble with boundaries is that it is not possible to see them, as if it was, it would allow other people to point out that they are missing. The help they need could then be provided, and there would be no reason for them to suffer for years on end.

If it was like physical pain, someone could go to the doctor and end up being diagnosed. Instead, they could end up being labelled in some way, and while this may allow them to move forward, it might also cause them to just stay where they are.

There is also the chance that they could end up having some kind of therapy, for instance, and once again, this could be a time when they end up dealing with the symptoms as opposed to the cause. Not only can this result in them wasting time and money, but it can also cause them to experience even more pain.

So, in the upcoming chapters, I will talk about some of the ways in which our life can be affected when we haven't developed any boundaries. In the last chapter, I will talk about what you can do in order to develop boundaries for the first time.

Boundaries – Are You Boundaryless?

Chapter 1

Anger

Do You Have Anger Problems?

While there are some people who get angry from time to time, there are others who are angry almost all of the time. Yet, this is not to say that there are only two categories, as there are going to be others who are rarely, if ever, angry.

When someone experiences life in this way, they could believe that there is no reason for them to get angry, and the people around them could see them as an inspiration. But even though someone who doesn't get angry can be seen as more developed than someone who is more or less always angry, it doesn't mean that this is necessarily the case.

A Reason

What this comes down to is that human beings have the ability to experience anger for a reason, and it could be said that the primary reason they can experience it is in order to protect themselves. So, whenever someone feels as though they are being taken advantage of or violated, it will be normal for them to experience anger.

Now, this is not to say that they need to be controlled by their anger; what it means is that it is important for them to be connected to this part of themselves. Through having this connection, they will be able to pay attention to the information that is being provided.

For Example

If someone is in touch with their anger and their boundaries are crossed, they would realise what has taken place. It would then be possible for them to take action, and this may mean that they have to step away from the situation and/or speak up, for instance.

However, if someone was not in touch with their anger, they might not even realise what has taken place. Thus, there would be no reason for them to do anything, and this could then mean that it would become normal for them to be walked over.

Containment

In the first example, someone who is not going to be controlled by their anger will simply pay attention to the information that is being provided. Another way of looking at this could be to say that their anger is contained.

But in the second example, there is going to be no reason for them to contain anything, and this is because they are not going to experience anger. What they could find, of course, is that they experience fear instead, and this will cause them to retract within themselves.

Sense of Self

As a result of this, they will lose themselves and end up being controlled by someone else. On the other hand, however, if someone can contain their anger, they are not going to lose themselves and they are not going to feel the need to control anyone else.

They will be maintaining their own boundaries and they will have no interest in trying to take advantage of anyone else. Alternatively, if one is unable to contain their anger, it could be normal for them to violate other people's boundaries.

The Opposite Experience

This is not to say that they won't experience fear like the person above; what it means is that they won't be in touch with this part of themselves. Through being overwhelmed by their anger, they will feel empowered.

They can then have no idea where they begin and end, and where other people begin and end. Through not being able to contain their anger, it will be a challenge for them to think clearly.

Regret

Once their anger has subsided, they may start to think about why they behaved as they did, and this could mean that they will experience regret. What could make it even harder for them to handle their behaviour is if it is something that takes place on a regular basis.

Having said that, there is also the chance that they won't experience regret at all, and this would show just how caught up they are. They could believe that they don't have any other choice, and then there will be no reason for them to feel bad about their behaviour.

One Option

However, if someone was aware of how destructive their behaviour is, and if they wanted to do something about it, they might end up looking into how they can control their anger. And while they could read a few books, they could also have some kind of therapy or coaching in order to achieve this.

During this time, they may come to believe that the reason they get so angry is because of what is taking place in their own head. Thus, in order for them to settle themselves down, it will be important for them to 'think differently'.

Exposed

After applying what they have learnt, they may find that they begin to settle down, and this will then allow them to carry on with their life. At the same time, they may find that this doesn't have much of an effect on them, and this could be a sign that they need to focus on their body as opposed to their mind.

If they were to take the time to connect with their body, they may find that they feel exposed, and through experiencing anger, this can stop them from feeling so vulnerable around others. If this is the case, it may mean that they haven't developed any boundaries.

Chapter 2

Anxiety

Do You Suffer From Anxiety?

It is not uncommon for someone to have anxiety problems in today's world, and while it may still be possible for them to carry on with the rest of their life relatively normally, there is also the chance that their whole life could end up being affected. In this case, it is going to be a challenge for them to enjoy their time on this earth.

Overactive

One way of looking at this would be to say that some people's anxiety is out of control, and this comes down to the fact that anxiety is something that everyone experiences to one degree or another. The primary difference is that not everyone's life is defined by it.

For some people, anxiety could be something that appears from time to time, and they may even be overwhelmed by it at certain times, but that could be as far as it goes. It is then not going to be something that consumes their whole life.

For Example

If someone had an exam coming up, or if they were about to go on a date, for instance, it would be normal for them to feel slightly anxious. Yet as time passes, this anxiety should soon disappear, and they will then be able to settle down.

When someone has an exam coming up, they can listen to how they feel, and it can then allow them to prepare in the right way. Yet if this

11

feedback didn't exist, it could cause them to overlook what they need to work on.

A Positive Influence

It could then be said that even though it may cause them to feel uncomfortable, it is not having a negative influence on their life. What is taking place within them then allows them to stay focused, and during moments such as these, it will be important for them to be aware of certain things.

However, if they experienced too much anxiety, this is likely to have a negative effect on their exam. For one thing, it will be hard for them to focus, and once they sit down to begin the exam, they could end up feeling completely overwhelmed.

Out of Control

This is different to when someone experiences anxiety for no apparent reason, and it may not matter if they are around others or by themselves, as they could still feel the same.

As a result of this, other people could see them as being unstable, and this could also cause them to feel uncomfortable in their presence. But, if they were to ask them why they were experiencing life in this way, they might not know what to say.

Avoidance

In order for them to take control of how they feel, they might end up avoiding certain situations, and while this might not have much of an impact on their life, it could cause them to actually sabotage their life.

When this happens, they may stop themselves from being able to live a full and fulfilling life.

But even though they may end up putting their life on hold, so to speak, it doesn't mean that they themselves will realise this. This is because they might be caught up in how they feel, and the most important thing could be for them to experience inner peace.

Conflict

At the same time, if someone is still in touch with their needs, they could end up experiencing inner conflict. On the one hand, they can feel the need to avoid certain situations, and on the other hand, they can feel the need to fulfil their own needs.

In this case, they might have moments when they are able to live as they would like to live, plus other moments when this is not at all possible. This could be how they have experienced life for a short time, or it could be something they have experienced for a number of years.

Reaching Out

Either way, it will be important for them to reach out for support, and through doing this, their life may gradually begin to change. One option would be to see their doctor, while another option would be to do an internet search.

If someone was to pay a visit to their doctor, the GP may refer them to some kind of therapist; however, there is also the chance that they will put them on some kind of medication instead. They could also go on medication and have therapy as well, and when this approach is taken, the medication they are on is usually used as just a short-term solution.

The Point of Focus

During this time, they can come to believe that their mind is defining how they feel. As a result, they may need to pay attention to their thoughts on the one hand, and to think differently on the other.

Through thinking differently, they may start to actually feel different, and this is because one's mind can define how they feel. It would be inaccurate to say that their mind always defines how they feel, as the mind can also be influenced by what is taking place in their body.

Another Angle

Therefore, if someone changes what is taking place in their mind but they still find that they are suffering from anxiety, they might need to focus on their body. For example, if someone doesn't feel safe in their body, it is going to be a challenge for their mind to settle down.

And because their body doesn't feel at ease, it might not matter what they do with their mind at all. If they were to try to change how they feel in their body through focusing on their mind, it could be the same as trying to warm up a meal by blowing hot air on it.

Not a Surprise

When someone doesn't feel safe in their own body, this can be a sign that they don't have any boundaries, and this is because boundaries would allow them to feel safe in their body. Without boundaries, it is not going to be much of a surprise if they have anxiety problems, and this is because they will probably feel exposed.

14

Chapter 3

Approval

Do You Worry About What Other People Think?

If someone hadn't learnt how to drive and they had to rely on someone else to drive them everywhere, their life will be a lot harder than it would be if they could drive. This is because they won't be able to go out when they want; they will only be able to go out when the other person is willing to take them out.

There will then be moments when they are able to do what they want to do, and other moments when this will not be the case. Having said that, if someone had their own personal driver, they would be able to go out whenever they wanted to.

Restricted

However, while this would be the ideal, it is not going to be an option for them, and this means that they are likely to feel restricted. And although they could be grateful that someone is there to help them, they could still experience a lot of frustration with the situation.

It is not going to be possible for them to lead the kind of life they want, and this will stop them from being able to grow. As they won't be able to go out when they want, it will also stop them from being able to have certain experiences.

Experiences

On the one hand, these could be experiences that they would have with their friends, while on the other hand, this can refer to what

15

would take place at a social event or on some kind of course. The kind of experiences they will miss out on will all depend on what their needs are.

However, even though someone's life can be limited through relying on another person to drive them everywhere, it is not the only way it can be limited. Another way that they can be held back is when they look to other people for approval.

Approval

Before they do anything, they will need other people to give them the all clear, so to speak, and once they can see that other people support their decision, they might be able to take action.

In this case, they are not waiting for someone else to give them a lift somewhere else, but they are still waiting for them to give them a mental and emotional lift. Without their support, they won't be able to take action, or if they do, they could do what they think other people want them to do rather than what they actually need.

Focus

Their point of focus is going to be on other people, and this could then mean that they are out of touch with their own needs and feelings. What this will show is that their primary concern is what other people think.

If other people say good things about them, they could end up feeling good about themselves, but if this is not the case, their mental and emotional state could soon start to change.

Walking On Egg Shells

It will be necessary for them to monitor their own behaviour, as this will be the only way for them to make sure they don't offend anyone. Another way of looking at this would be to say that they will be walking on egg shells.

They may believe that as long as they don't offend anyone, they won't have to suffer. Yet through doing this, it is not going to be possible for them to express their true-self; therefore, their whole life could actually become an expression of their false-self.

Feedback

This doesn't necessarily mean that other people will realise what is taking place, as they could see them as being easy-going. It is then not that they are out of touch with themselves; it is that they are happy to be there for others.

At the same time, there could be people who say they don't stand up for themselves, and they may believe that they are *too* easy-going. They may say that the only way they will experience true fulfilment is if they stop caring about what other people think.

Balance

One way of looking at this would be to say that it is important to be open to feedback from others, but that doesn't mean that someone should let them define their own life. Of course, they would also experience problems if they were unable to listen to feedback from others.

It could be said that the ideal would be for someone to live their life whilst being able to listen to what other people have to say, without it taking over their own life. This feedback can then play an important part in their growth and development.

Only Words

If they were to talk to someone about what is taking place for them, they may be told that they don't need to worry about what other people think – they are only words and it is not possible to be hurt by them.

Along with this, they could say that it is not as if they are being physically attacked, and that what others say is only their opinion. They could then be told that they need to change what they believe and to start thinking differently, for instance.

Wide Open

Still, even though they are only words, they could feel as though they go straight through them. As a result, they are not going to simply hear these things; they will feel as though their very survival is at risk.

What this will then show is that they are boundaryless, and this means that they are wide open at an energetic level. Thus, it is not so much about what is taking place in their mind as it is about what is taking place in their body.

Chapter 4

Empathy

Do You Experience Too Much Empathy?

There can be times when someone has too much of something, and other times when they don't have enough. It is often said that when someone wants something it is never there, and yet when they don't want it, it ends up appearing.

However, while this can relate to something physical, it is also something that can relate to someone's personality. For example, someone can be in a position where they have come to the conclusion that they are out of balance.

The Reason

This could be a sign that they have reflected on their own behaviour, or it could be the result of what other people have said to them. At the same time, both of these factors may have had an influence.

Perhaps they have had this outlook for only a number of days, or it may have been something they have had for a number of years. Still, there is going to be a strong chance that they want to do something about it and not just carry on as they are.

Empathy

If they were to think about what is causing them to suffer, they may find that it is to do with their ability to experience other people's emotional states. In this case, something that should actually enhance their life is having the opposite effect.

19

And the reason it is having a negative effect on their life is likely to come down to the fact that it is something that causes them to be overwhelmed. It is then not a case of simply tuning into another person's emotional state before tuning out again; it is something that takes over their whole being.

The Other Extreme

How they experience life is then going to be completely different to someone who doesn't have the ability to empathise with others or is only able to do this at certain times. If anything, it could be said that it would be a good idea for them to work on their ability to tune into other people's emotional states.

It might then be normal for them to be told that they are cold, or that they appear to be lacking something. Yet, regardless of the kind of feedback that they get from others, they are not going to be overwhelmed by how other people feel.

In The Middle

There are then going to be people who have the ability to tune into other people's emotional states without being overwhelmed. Now, this is not to say that this will always be the way, but it is likely to be what generally takes place.

Through being like this, having the ability to empathise will be something that has a positive effect on their life. Their relationships are likely to be more fulfilling than they would be if they didn't have this ability, and it will also be a lot easier for them to experience intimacy.

A Way of Life

When someone experiences too much empathy, it will be normal for them to lose touch with how they feel. In fact, they might find it hard to work out whether how they feel relates to their own emotional state or to someone else's.

To experience life in this way is going to be incredibly draining, and they may feel the need to spend a lot of time by themselves. Through doing this, it may allow them to settle themselves down.

Day-To-Day Life

On the one hand, there will be the challenges that they have to face in their personal relationships, and on the other hand, there will be what takes place in their day-to-day life. When they spend time with their friends and family, for instance, they could end up being drawn into their experience.

Yet this is something that could take place whilst they are at work or if they were to go shopping as well. Thus, being around others is going to be something that takes a lot from them and doesn't give them much in return.

A Common Dynamic

If they were to have intimate relationships with others, they may find that they end up with people who don't have the same amount of empathy as they do. In fact, they may attract people who are unable to experience empathy at all.

These people are then going to be a complete mismatch, and they are going to end up giving far more than they receive. These could be the kinds of relationships that are typically seen as being abusive.

Needs

So, as their point of awareness is generally going to be on how other people feel, it is going to be a challenge for them to get their needs met. But, as they are so caught up in other people's lives, they might not even know what their needs are.

One way of looking at this would be to say that even though they are physically separate from others, it is still not possible for them to have their own experience. They will feel wide open, and unless this changes, they will continue to soak up what is taking place around them.

Overly Sensitive

It could be said that they are sensitive, and that this is something they have to put up with, and while this could be the case, there could be more to it. What it could come down to is that they are boundaryless, and this is then why they absorb so much.

Chapter 5

Intimacy

Do You Find It Hard To Experience Intimacy?

For some people, experiencing intimacy will be a normal part of life, and it is then not going to be something that they will need to worry about. If this wasn't the case, however, and they were unable to experience intimacy at all, it could be something that ends up consuming their whole life.

Their need to experience a deeper connection with others is not being met, and this is likely to have an effect on every other area of their life. What this shows is how strong this need is, and how it is not something that can simply be overlooked.

Interdependent

Another way of looking at this is to say that human beings are interdependent; they don't just want others, they *need* others. On one level, someone can share their mind; on another level, they can share their body; and on another level still, they can share their heart.

If the only thing someone shared with others was their mind, they are unlikely to feel connected to their fellow human beings. The same could also be said if they had moments where they only shared their body.

The Defining Factor

What will make the difference is when they share their heart with others; when this happens, they will be talking about their feelings, among other things. Therefore, their mind will also be used, but they won't need to be using their body.

So, while someone can use their body when they are being intimate, it is not something that always needs to occur. If one could only be intimate through using their body, it wouldn't be possible for them to be intimate with friends and family, for instance.

Less Pressure

Through being able to experience intimacy with more than one person, it will make their life easier. For instance, if they only looked towards one person, it would put a lot of pressure on them, and if the relationship was to come to an end, this could cause a lot of problems.

However, when someone has a number of different people in their life that they can open up to, there will be less pressure on the person they are with. If one relationship was to come to an end, they would still have other people to share their feelings with.

Another Outlook

When intimacy is seen as something that can only take place in an intimate relationship, it is going to be a lot harder for that person to be single. Also, during the moments when they are with someone, they might end up expecting too much from them.

This is not to say that it is possible for someone to experience the same kind of connection with a friend or a family member as they would in an intimate relationship, as it is going to be very different. What it comes down to is that someone can be intimate with more than one person.

24

Intimacy

If someone does experience intimacy, it could be how their life has been for many years. As a result, they might not know what it is like to experience life differently.

There can then be others who used to experience life differently and, through putting in the work, they were able to change their experience of life. Based on how their life is, it could now be seen as normal, but based on their life as a whole, it is a relatively new experience.

The Contrast

Through living without intimacy, they will know how much of a difference it makes to experience it. Before this, they may have felt disconnected from others, and that other people had something they didn't have.

This may have caused them to feel like a victim from time to time, or they may even have had a victim mentality. Yet, no matter how they felt, they were not prepared to tolerate what was taking place.

One Side

However, even if someone is unable to experience intimacy, it doesn't mean they have never been close to another person. There may have been moments in their life where this has happened, but it might not have lasted for very long.

This could mean that they have a pattern of attracting people who are not available. In this case, another person could be in their life, but just as they start to experience a connection, they could soon disappear.

The Other Side

Along with this, they may have had moments where people were available but they didn't find them attractive. They could then come to believe that the only way for them to experience intimacy will be for them to be with someone who they don't want to be with.

There is also the chance that they have ended up feeling overwhelmed when someone has been in their life. This could then be a sign that they only feel comfortable when other people are kept at a certain distance.

Conflict

What this is likely to show is that even though they want to get close to others, it is something that doesn't quite feel right. Experiencing intimacy can then be seen as something that will cause them to lose themselves.

The need to survive is stronger than the need to experience intimacy, and this is why someone may not be able to experience intimacy unless they feel that it is safe for them to do so. But unless they realise why they are unable to experience intimacy, they can end up feeling as though they have no control over this part of their life whatsoever.

A Safe Distance

What this is likely to show is that they haven't developed boundaries, and this is why they don't feel comfortable getting close to others.

Their body is then going to feel exposed during these moments, and it will become normal for them to do everything they can to keep their distance.

Chapter 6

Isolation

Do You Isolate Yourself?

On the one hand, there are said to be people who like to spend a lot of time around others, and on the other, there are said to be people who don't. Another way of looking at this would be to say that there are extroverts and introverts.

But while some people will see themselves in this way, there are also going to be people who don't. If they were asked how they would describe themselves, they might not be able to identity with either of these two terms.

A Bit of Both

They could say that there are times in their life when they want to be around others and times in their life when this is not the case. As a result of this, it would be inaccurate to say that they are either an extrovert or an introvert.

However, this is not to say that they will want to spend as much time with others as they do by themselves. There is the chance that they will prefer to spend more time with others than they do in their own company, or vice versa.

Different Periods

Also, this doesn't mean that their needs will always be the same, as there could be certain periods in their life when they need to experience life differently. During these moments, they may find that

29

they need to be around others more, or they could take a step back because they need to spend less time around others.

It could be said that this is a normal part of life, and how it is to be expected that someone's needs are not always going to stay the same. There are a number of reasons as to why this is.

The Reasons

It is often said that the sun brings people out, and so one may prefer to go out more when it's warmer. Thus, during the colder months, they may end up having less contact with other people.

What can also play a part here is if one has gone through a break-up, or if a loved one has passed on. This could be something that brings them in, or they may end up needing more stimulation than they usually do.

Months or Years

If someone has the need to take a step back from how they used to be, they may find that it is only a matter of months before they feel the need to be around others again. At the same time, this might not be long enough, and they may end up being this way for a year or more.

What this shows is that not everyone is the same, and just because someone responds differently to something, it doesn't mean there is anything wrong with them. It simply shows that they are responding differently, and during this time, it will be important for them to be compassionate towards themselves.

One Side

However, even though someone can be in a position where they prefer less contact with others, they can also be in a position where they do everything they can to avoid it. And, when they are around others, they may or may not have a lot to say.

The only time they feel comfortable could be when they are by themselves. This could be how they have been for as long as they can remember, or it might be a fairly recent occurrence.

Normal

When someone has experienced life in this way for quite some time, they might not even think about why they are this way. It could just be seen as who they are, and the people around them could also see it as a reflection of their personality, for instance.

But if they were to think about why they behave in this way, it could cause them to end up feeling angry. They could see people who *do* embrace life and wonder what it would be like. Another way of saying this is that they may look up to the people who experience life differently from them.

A Recent Occurrence

On the other hand, if someone has only just started to behave in this way, it might be hard for them to understand what is going on. As a result of this, the people around them could also wonder why they have changed.

If they were to think about what is going on, or if someone else was to ask them, they might not be able to find an answer. Part of them will then have the need to hide and another part of them will have the need to embrace life.

Conflict

The part of them that is the strongest is likely to be the part of them that wants to hide, and this will cause them to experience conflict. When someone behaves in this way, it is going to mean that a lot of their needs end up being overlooked.

In fact, they could be so concerned with avoiding others that they don't even think about their other needs, but unless they are able to feel comfortable around others, this is something that is not going to change.

A Way to Feel Safe

What this can show is that they are boundaryless, and this is why they don't feel comfortable around others. Their body will feel exposed, and avoiding others will be a way for them to feel safe.

Chapter 7

People Pleasing

Do You Have The Need To Please Others?

In today's world, it is not uncommon for someone to hear about how they shouldn't be a people pleaser. This may have been something they have come into contact with through reading books on self-development, or they may have heard about it after reading articles online, for instance.

If this wasn't the case, it may have been something they've heard from the people they know. Nevertheless, someone may find that they have the same outlook, and this could then be a sign that they are not a people pleaser.

The Right Outlook

When someone thinks about being a people pleaser, they may think about how it wouldn't be possible for them to live their own life. And perhaps that they would always have to neglect their own needs in order to fulfil other people's needs.

If someone was to reflect on their own life, they may find that they have been this way for as long as they can remember. At the same time, there may have been a time in their life when they *were* a people pleaser.

Pain

Through experiencing life in this way, they are going to be only too aware of what it is like to always focus on other people's needs, and

33

this is likely to mean that they experienced a lot of pain during this time.

However, this is not to say that other people always realised that they were ignoring their own needs. The reason for this is that the person may have come across as though they had it all together, and this would have stopped a lot of people from seeing what was really taking place.

Career

For example, someone may have been in a position where they had a very successful career, and this may have meant that certain people saw them as an example to follow. Along with this, they may have acted as though they were doing something they enjoyed, even if they weren't.

While this is how they came across to others, it may have been a different story when they were by themselves. Yet, if this wasn't the case, it may have been because they avoided their true feelings, and this could have meant that they had a number of escapes.

Waking Up

Still, regardless of what was taking place in their life, they were able to step back and see that they were on the wrong track. This is not to say that this happened overnight, but it could have been something that occurred.

And although part of them may have been in a place of resistance, another part of them may no longer have been prepared to experience life in the same way. During this time, they may have had people who supported them, as well as people who didn't.

Loss

They may have thought about how – even though they would probably lose a few people – it was something that was worth doing, and perhaps they came to this conclusion through thinking about how it wasn't possible for them to be themselves.

It was then a case of either putting other people's happiness first, or putting their own happiness first. Based on this, it wouldn't have been possible for them to avoid loss; it was more about what they were prepared to lose in order to live a more fulfilling life.

Support

In order for them to get from where they were to where they are, they may have reached out for support. This could have been provided through the books that they read, for instance, or they may have worked with another person.

What this all comes down to is that there is no such thing as a 'one size fits all' approach, and this is because there can be a number of reasons as to why someone would behave in a certain way. This is partly why self-understanding is so important, as it will give someone the chance to find out what approach they need to take.

A Way of Life

However, even though someone could agree with the outlook above, it doesn't mean that they are able to pay attention to their own needs. On the one hand, they will have the desire to fulfil their own needs, while on the other hand, they will feel the desire to always fulfil other people's needs.

The part of them that is the strongest is going to be the part that always feels the need to please other people. As a result of this, they could feel as though they have no control over their life, and they may find that they are used to feeling like a victim.

Self-Expression

Therefore, no matter how they come across to other people, it is not going to be possible for them to live their own life. Their life is not only going to be an expression of what other people want it to be; it will also be an expression of what they *think* other people want it to be like.

They could find that there are moments in their life when they don't even know what their needs are. In fact, this could be something that they have become accustomed to, and this is to be expected; especially as they are so concerned with other people's needs.

Moving Forward

Now, if one was to reach out for support with this, they may be told that they need to look into what is taking place in their own mind. They could come across information that goes into how they need to change what they believe, and they may hear about how it will be important for them to work on their 'self-esteem', among other things.

Through taking this approach, one may find that their need for approval gradually begins to diminish. Yet at the same time, they may find that even though they have worked on their mind, they still don't feel comfortable putting their own needs first.

Self-Expression

If this is the case, the reason why someone doesn't feel comfortable putting their needs first could be because they are boundaryless. Through feeling so exposed, it will be normal for them to feel that it is not safe for them to live their own life.

Chapter 8

Receiving

Do You Find it Hard To Receive?

If someone was to drive somewhere that wasn't too far away, they wouldn't need to have a lot of fuel in their car. However, if they wanted to go somewhere that was over an hour away, for instance, this wouldn't be the case.

But as long as they took the time to get the fuel they needed, this wouldn't be a problem. Having said that, if it wasn't possible for them to put fuel in their car at all, they simply wouldn't be able to get there.

The Only Option

The only thing they would be able to do in this case would be to go somewhere locally, or to stay at home. In this sense, it could be said that they will have to compromise, and this is not going to be as fulfilling.

Now, if this was something that only took place from time to time, it might not bother them, but if it was to happen *all* the time, it would be harder for them to handle. What would also make this harder to handle was if their car had run out of fuel, stopping them from going anywhere.

Everyday Life

This is similar to how one can suffer when they are unable to receive what they need to receive in life. On the one hand, this can mean that they are able to receive from time to time, and on the other hand, it can mean that this is something that rarely takes place.

As a result of this, their life is going to be a lot harder than it needs to be, and this could mean that they are used to suffering in one way or another. Yet, even though they are unable to receive, it doesn't mean that they realise this about themselves.

One Outlook

Instead, someone can believe that they are unlucky or less fortunate than others, and this can then mean that they see themselves as a victim. It is not that they *can't* receive; it is that the world is stopping them from being able to have their needs met.

Their outlook could be supported by some of the people they spend time with, as well as the other people they come across during their life. If someone supports their outlook, it could be because they experience life in the same way.

Random

However, if that is not the case, it could be a sign that they believe people have very little control when it comes to how they experience life. So, if someone is in a position where they get their needs met, they could believe that they are one of the lucky ones.

Thus, it will be normal for them to see people who experience life differently as being the unlucky ones. Therefore, while someone like this will be able to display empathy, they are not going to be able to assist them.

Alternatively

At the same time, someone could have moments when they feel like a victim, and moments when they don't. And, when they don't feel as though they have any control over their life, they could realise that they are playing a part in what is happening.

During this time, they may wonder why part of them wants to receive and another part of them doesn't. In general, they could find that the part of them that doesn't want to receive is the strongest part.

Overwhelmed

When this part of them takes over, they may find that they end up feeling overwhelmed when they receive something. Or, they could feel this way when there is only the chance that this is something that may take place.

This could also mean that they prefer to keep people at a certain distance, and they may also prefer to spend time by themselves. But if they are able to settle down, this may soon change, and they could then be drawn to others.

Relationships

Another way of looking at this would be to say that it can have a negative effect on their relationships, which could mean that it is not possible for them to experience intimacy.

Other Areas

Along with this, one could also find that they can only get so far when it comes to their career, and on a deeper level, this can be seen as something else that will cause them to experience too much pressure.

For one thing, they will have to commit to certain things and to have experiences that will cause them to lose themselves. Through not being able to embrace life, so to speak, it can also have an effect on their ability to be supported financially.

Conflict

Being able to receive is a vital part of life, and this is why it can be hard for someone to understand why it would be such a problem. However, if someone feels overwhelmed when they receive, it can be normal for them to keep life at bay.

The trouble is that while this can feel comfortable, it can also cause them to suffer unnecessarily. What this can then show is that one doesn't feel safe in their own body, and this then sets them up to reject life.

Resistance

As a result of this, they are not going to be able to receive, and this is likely to show that they are boundaryless. At an energetic level, they are going to be completely exposed, and unless this changes, their life is unlikely to change either.

Chapter 9

Relationships

Do You Lose Yourself In A Relationship?

While some people can maintain their sense of self in a relationship, there are others who are unable to do so. As a result, their experiences are going to be radically different from others, and this could be how they have been for most of their life.

A Big Difference

When someone is able to maintain their sense of self, it will give them the chance to meet their own needs. Along with this, they will also be able to meet the other person's needs, and this means that the relationship will be in balance.

However, when someone is unable to maintain their sense of self, there is going to be less chance of their needs being met. Instead, they could find that they end up being focused on the other person's needs, and the relationship will then be out of balance.

In Touch

In the first example, someone is going to be in touch with their needs, and in the second example, they might be out of touch with their needs. Being aware of their needs will be one part; the other part will be feeling comfortable enough to reveal them to others.

When someone is focused on the other person's needs, they might be aware of their own needs from time to time, but it might not matter to them. This is primarily because they are unlikely to feel comfortable enough to reveal them to the other person.

Self-Acceptance

When someone accepts themselves, they are likely to feel comfortable with their own needs, and this will allow them to receive. Therefore, they are not going to believe that something 'bad' will happen by opening up.

Yet, when someone doesn't accept themselves, it is going to be a challenge for them to open up. If they were to do this, they may believe that something 'bad' would take place.

The Priority

It could then be said that they are more concerned with pleasing the other person than they are about pleasing themselves. Now, being aware of the other person's needs is not bad per se; but if someone is completely out of touch with their own needs, it is going to cause them to suffer.

When this happens, it will not be a case of someone fulfilling the other person's needs from time to time; they will always be fulfilling their needs. Through being out of touch with their own needs, they could feel as though they are doing the right thing.

Selfless

They could then be seen as someone who is 'selfless', and as long as the other person is happy, that could be enough. Their point of focus is then on the other person, meaning they may not be aware of what is taking place within them.

This is not to say they will always be happy, as there could be moments when they feel down. They could also end up coming across as being passive aggressive, and this could be because they don't feel comfortable opening up about what is going on.

Conflict

On the one hand, pleasing the other person could be what feels right, but on the other, it may also cause them to feel uncomfortable. It can then be strange for them to understand why this would cause them to feel uncomfortable; especially when it allows them to be accepted by the other person.

This doesn't mean, however, that the relationship will be healthy, as it could mean that the other person takes advantage of them. And, if someone is primarily focused on being accepted, they might overlook what is actually taking place.

Normal

Regardless of how they are treated by the other person, this is likely to be what they consider normal, and while it would be easy to blame the other person, this is not something that is out of their control. Based on how they are experiencing life, they could believe that they have no control over what is happening.

In order for them to see life differently, it will be important for them to experience an internal shift. Unless this takes place, they will expect the other person to change, and this could cause them to feel like a victim.

Sense of Self

If they were to take a step back and think about what is happening, they might come to see that they lose themselves when they are with the other person. They are then no longer an individual; they are simply an extension of someone else.

The other person's behaviour could be seen as the reason why this happens, but if this is something that has happened before, there is probably going to be more to it. On a deeper level, this could be what feels safe to them, and unless this changes, their life is also unlikely to change.

Boundaryless

When one can maintain their sense of self in a relationship, it is likely to be a sign that they feel safe in their own body. Yet, when someone doesn't feel safe in their body, this will cause them to leave their body, and their attention will then be on their mind.

As a result, it will be normal for them to focus on the other person, and this is because they will be out of touch with the needs and feelings that are in their own body. If they had boundaries, they wouldn't need to experience life in this way.

Chapter 10

Saying No

Do You Find It Hard To Say No?

If someone is given the opportunity to do something, it will be up to them to decide if they want to go along with it. This is not to say that they can't talk to other people about it; what it means is that they are the only ones who know if it is right for them or not.

They could be in a position where they are ready to embrace the opportunity that is in front of them, and it is then not going to be necessary for them to think about it for a while, or to get other people's views on it. And, after they have made their decision, they are likely to believe that they have done the right thing.

A Choice

Through having this outlook, it could be said that they didn't say yes because they had to; they said yes because they wanted to. This could mean that they generally behave in this way, and it could then be said that they are able to stand their ground in life.

As they are able to say yes, there is also the chance that they are able to say no, and this means that they have the right balance. For one thing, it is often said that being able to say no is more important than being able to say yes.

The Reason

When someone says yes, it can mean that they are going along with what someone else wants; whereas when they say no, it can mean that they are not going along with what someone else wants. In the first instance, someone can end up receiving approval, and in the second instance, they can end up losing out on this approval.

Therefore, they can be under a lot more pressure when they say 'no' than when they say 'yes', and this is why it can be a lot harder for them to say 'no'. In general, the easiest thing one can do is to say yes.

Approval

This is why it is important for someone to be in a position where they don't have a strong need for approval. If they *do* have a strong need for approval and they want to change the ways in which they experience life, they could talk to someone who is able to say no.

During this time, they may tell them that nothing bad will happen if they do, and that if they value themselves, it will be the obvious thing for them to do. And through being able to say no, they may tell themselves that this will allow them to say yes.

More Than a Word

This is not to say that they can't already say 'yes'; what it comes down to is that it will mean something when they say it. On the other hand, if they were only able to say 'yes', it would be meaningless.

Thus, when people hear the word 'yes', they will know that they are not just saying it. However, if they hadn't heard them say 'no', it might not be possible for them to have this outlook.

Needs

Ultimately, when someone has the ability to use both words, it will allow them to pay attention to their own needs. And, through being able to pay attention to them, it will give them the chance to fulfil these needs.

Through having this ability, their life is going to be far more fulfilling than it would be if this wasn't the case. Now, this is not to say that everyone will approve of their behaviour, but this is just a part of life.

Support

The people who will support them are likely to be the ones they are close to, and this is because they are likely to have the same outlook as them. They will expect their friends to be honest, and in turn, their friends will expect them to be honest as well.

At the same time, this doesn't mean that it will necessarily be this way with their family members. If this is the case, it could be due to the fact that their family expects them to say yes all the time.

Loss

Regardless of this, they are not going to be prepared to lose themselves in order to please their entire family, or just a certain family member. What this shows is that no matter what they do, they will lose something.

And, through valuing themselves, it will be possible for them to make sure that they don't have a tendency to ignore their own needs.

Another Experience

If someone does have a strong need for approval and they speak to someone who tells them it is OK for them to stand their ground, they may find that their life soon changes. Or, if this doesn't take place and they were to read up on how they need to be more assertive, for instance, they could also experience a similar outcome.

During this time, they are primarily going to be focused on what is taking place in their own mind, as well as focusing on their own behaviour. However, while this approach may work for some people, it is not going to work for everyone.

Exposed

Someone could find that they only feel safe when they do what other people want (or what they think they want), and this is likely to be a sign that they don't feel safe. Pleasing other people is then going to be a way for them to protect themselves.

If they were to get in touch with their body, they may find that they feel exposed, and this is then likely to mean that they are boundaryless. What this shows is that they haven't been able to develop an energetic boundary, so it will then be normal for them to feel wide open.

Chapter 11

Sense of Self

Do You Lose Yourself Around Others?

While some people are able to maintain their sense of self when they are around others, there are going to be other people who are unable to do so. However, even though this is what is taking place, it doesn't mean that someone will necessarily realise what is happening.

Part of Life

For example, if someone can maintain their sense of self, it could be what is normal to them. It is then not something they ever think about; it is just part of their life.

In this case, they may have experienced life in this way for most of their years, and because of this, they might not realise that not everyone experiences life in this way. This is not to say they won't ever lose themselves, but it could happen so rarely that it doesn't have an impact on them.

Under Pressure

If it does happen, it could be something that takes place during a stressful period of their life. For instance, if they were to lose their job or they were to experience the end of a relationship, they might lose touch with themselves for a short time.

Along with this, they might experience a similar occurrence if they were to go on a date, but in this case, it might only be a momentary experience. However, regardless of why they experience life differently, it shouldn't be long until they return to how they were before.

Two Occurrences

Through experiencing life in this way, it could cause them to reflect on how their life would be if they were like that all the time. As a result, they might experience a sense of gratitude and think about how fortunate they are.

At the same time, they might look back on what happened and wonder why they behaved as they did. Depending on what happened, they could end up feeling angry about it, or they might even start to laugh.

Life Goes On

Whether or not this happens, they are likely to carry on with their life, and this will be a life where they have a real sense of self. This means that not only will they be in touch with their own needs and feelings when they are around others, but they will also be able to express them.

Therefore, they won't need to overlook what is taking place within themselves, or get caught up with what is taking place around them. This is not to say that they won't be able to respond to other people's needs; what it means is that they won't act as though they are an extension of other people.

Connected

Along with being connected to themselves, they will also feel that it is safe for them to be themselves. How they behave around the people they are close to will generally be a reflection of their true-self.

This means that they are able to experience intimacy with others, and this is because they will be able to share what is taking place within them. However, whilst they might enjoy being approved of by others, it is not going to define their behaviour.

Self-Expression

Through being able to be themselves around others, it is likely to mean that their life will be an expression of their true needs. Whereas if someone was unable to be themselves around others, their life is likely to be a reflection of how other people want it to be.

What is true for them could end up being ignored, and their life could end up becoming an expression of what is true for others. It is then not possible for them to please themselves; they will be more concerned about pleasing others.

Identity

Other people could see them as easy-going, or they may say, for instance, that they lack confidence. How they behave may depend on who they are with, but this is not the same as having the ability to adjust around different people.

What this can mean is that they will disconnect from themselves and end up being defined solely by the people they are with. They are then out of touch with their true-self, and this may appear to be something that 'just happens'.

A Door Mat

It can then be normal for them to do things they don't want to do, and while this might cause them to experience frustration, it could be far worse. This is because they could end up being abused by others.

However, just because they are being compromised, it doesn't mean that they will let anyone know. They might not believe that they can do anything about what is taking place.

Overwhelmed

Although they will have the need to be themselves around others, this could be something that doesn't seem possible. Being around others could cause them to feel overwhelmed, and it is then going to be a challenge for them to experience life differently.

But even though their behaviour around others doesn't always reflect their true-self, it doesn't mean that others will realise this; other people could see it as being who they really are, and this could make them feel even more restricted.

A Closer Look

In order for someone to be able to maintain their sense of self around others, they will need to feel safe in their own body. If they don't, it can be normal for them to leave their body and to live in their head, or to dissociate from themselves.

When they are in their head, they will be focused on others, and they won't be able to express themselves. Whereas if they felt safe in their body, they wouldn't need to focus on others and they could then express their true-self.

Normal

What this is likely to show is that they haven't developed any boundaries; if they had, they would be able to feel safe being in their body. Through not having boundaries, it is to be expected that they will feel exposed.

Chapter 12

Skin

Do You Have Skin Problems?

In the past, if someone was to see perfect skin, it may have been because they were looking at images in a magazine; however, if they were to come across perfect skin in today's world, it could be because they are using social media. And, as one can use social media whenever they like, it also means that they can see perfect skin whenever they like.

But, while someone might realise that the only reason why another's skin would look perfect in a magazine is because it has been edited, it doesn't mean they would realise that the same process could take place on social media. As a result of this, it could cause them to believe that it is normal to have perfect skin.

Reading Between the Lines

It could be said that although there will be times when people do have perfect skin, there will also be times when they don't. Along with this, there are likely to be plenty of people who rarely have good skin.

When one has this outlook, they might not feel the need to always have perfect skin. For one thing, they will know that this is not always going to be possible, and this realisation can make it a lot easier for them to feel good about themselves.

Acceptance

If someone believes that their skin should always be flawless, they will end up setting themselves up to suffer unnecessarily. While it is going to be easy for someone's skin to look flawless in a magazine or on social media, it won't be as easy in the real world.

They can't simply press a few buttons and transform their skin; the only option they may have is to use something on their face. For a woman, this could be make-up, and for a man, this could be some kind of moisturiser.

A Long-Term Solution

These options could provide a short-term solution; however, if someone really wanted to improve their skin, it will be important for them to take a closer look at their life – for instance, they may find that they need to change their diet, and/or they may need to get more sleep.

It might also be important for them to look into how they feel each day, as they might be experiencing too much stress. Through looking into each of these areas and making the necessary changes, their skin may start to improve.

The Key Area

The area that someone is most concerned about (when it comes to their skin) could be their face, because this is the area that everybody sees. There would then be their neck, hands, and arms.

If they lived in a hot country and had the need to wear less clothing, it would also include other areas of their body. On top of this, when someone is in a relationship or if they just share their body with another person, they are also going to reveal more.

A Profession

Someone could also have a profession where their body is on show, and it will then be even more important for them to look after their skin. It won't be enough for them to just look after the skin on their face either; they will need to look after the skin on every part of their body.

On the one hand, someone might be in a position where they struggle with spots, while on the other hand, they might be in a position where they suffer from dry skin. If they can relate to the former, it may mean that their skin is not painful, but if they can relate to the latter, it may mean that their skin *is* painful.

A Common Approach

If someone has skin that is painful, there is a chance that they will go to see their doctor, and one approach might be for them to go onto some kind of antibiotics. During this time, they are likely to be asked how long their skin has been like this.

They might also be asked about their skin care routine, and their diet might be another area that is looked into. Through taking this approach, they may find that it is only a matter of time before their skin starts to heal.

Another Factor

Along with this, they could also look into what was taking place in their life when their skin started to change. Of course, if their skin has been like this for quite some time, it might prove harder for them to do this.

It will be important for them to look into what was taking place around them on the one hand, and to look into what was taking place within them on the other. This is because although someone can have experiences in their life that are stressful, they can also experience stress due to what is taking place within themselves.

Both Ways

What this shows is that there is not just what happens – there is also how someone responds to what happens. Also, if someone feels stressed on the inside, they can end up creating experiences that mirror how they feel.

This is why it will be important for them to look into what has been taking place around them as well as what has been taking place within them. When someone has skin problems, it can be a sign that their boundaries are being crossed.

Violation

Not only do boundaries give someone the ability to say yes and no; they also allow one to feel safe in their own body. When someone doesn't feel as though it is safe for them to exist, they are likely to feel exposed.

Their energetic boundary is then not going to exist, and because of this it can be normal for them to feel as though other people are getting under their skin, so to speak. As a result of this, they might not feel safe enough to speak their truth.

Anger

Through being walked over, one is likely to end up feeling angry; but as they already don't feel safe, they can end up disconnecting from how they feel. This energy then has to go somewhere, and one place it can go to is one's skin.

The cracks that appear can then be seen as a sign that something is trying to get out, and what is trying to get out can be the emotional energy that has built up within them.

Chapter 13

True-Self

Do You Find it Hard To Express Your True-Self?

On the one hand, someone could be in a position where they are able to express their true-self, and on the other hand, they could be in a position where this isn't the case. At the same time, they could also find that it is possible for them to do this, but only from time to time.

If this is the case, it is likely to mean that they can only express themselves around certain people and during certain situations, and this is no doubt going to have a negative effect on their life. So, whether someone is unable to be themselves, or if they can only do this on the odd occasion, it is going to cause them to suffer.

Part of Life

There is the chance that they will have experienced life in this way for as long as they can remember, and this could then mean that they have come to believe that there is nothing they can do. If this is the case, it will cause them to suffer, but that will be as far as it goes.

However, someone could also find that they are unwilling to experience life in this way for much longer, and this may cause them to look for answers. It could then be said that they are taking a more proactive approach.

Depressed

When someone doesn't take this approach and continues to experience life in the same way, they will be just be tolerating what is taking place. As a result of this, they could end up seeing themselves as a victim.

And while they may be used to feeling angry, they may also have moments when they feel depressed. This can be a reflection of the fact that they feel as though they have no control over what is happening in their life.

A Symptom

But, even though they only feel depressed because they can't express their true-self, it doesn't mean that they will actually realise this. This can mean that they will end up trying to treat a symptom as opposed to the cause.

Through taking this approach, they could end up feeling better even though their life hasn't changed. One way of looking at this would be to say that they have lost touch with the feedback that they need in order to change their life.

Feedback

The pain that they were experiencing was not bad per se; it was simply there to let them know that something wasn't right. So, through removing this pain, it will stop them from being aware of the fact that something isn't right.

This will then stop them from being able to change their life, but while it would be easy to say that they have the wrong approach, they are simply a product of their environment – in today's world, pain is often seen as something that needs to be removed, and not as something that needs to be understood.

The False-Self

And, if someone is living in a way that goes against who they are, it is to be expected that they will end up suffering in one way or another. In this sense, the pain they are experiencing can be seen as their ally as opposed to their enemy.

When they are around others, they will be likely to find that they generally behave how other people want them to behave, or how they think they want them to behave. Thus, their own needs and feelings are going to end up being overlooked.

Disconnected

They will then be aware of what is taking place within them, but that will be as far as it goes. And, when they are no longer around others, they could end up wondering why they were unable to be themselves.

On the other hand, they could also be out of touch with what is taking place within them, and this could even be the case when they are by themselves. During this time, they could just feel angry and down, without knowing why.

Another Consequence

This could also mean that it is not possible for them to have a fulfilling career, and even if they are doing something that *is* fulfilling, they may find that they can only get so far with it. If they were able to express themselves, it would be a lot easier for them to move forward.

Approval

And, if they were to really think about why they behave as they do, they may find that they need other people's approval. As a result, they may believe that their life would soon change if this was no longer the case.

Based on this, if they were to reach out for support, they may look for a way to let go of this need. This could then be a time where they will change what they believe, and they could even begin to think differently.

The Body

However, while someone's life could change through placing their attention on their mind, this might not be enough. They could find that the reason they are unable to express their true-self is because they don't feel safe.

Therefore, it could be a sign that they need to focus on their body and not their mind. If they were to get in touch with their body, they may feel as though they were exposed, and it could then be said that they are boundaryless.

Chapter 14

Ungrounded

Do You Find It Hard to Stay In Your Body?

If someone was to say that they were leaving their job or a relationship, there is a strong chance that other people would know what they were talking about. For instance, when they think about what someone is doing, they might imagine them saying goodbye to their colleagues or walking away from the person they were with.

Through being in this position, there is the chance that they will be able to empathise with them. Along with this, they may also tell them that they are there for them if they need their support.

Normal

It could be said that it is normal for someone to receive these kinds of responses, and this is because they are talking about something that most people can relate to. As it is so common, they may also find that there are people in their life that are having a similar experience, or that this may have been the case just a short while ago.

However, if someone was to tell another person that they were leaving something or someone and they didn't understand, it could be because they are not very old. Or it could mean that the person they are talking to speaks another language.

Support

When someone talks about something and other people can understand what they are talking about, it is going to make their life a whole lot easier. However, while other people can understand them when they talk about these kinds of things, this is not always going to be the case.

Now, this isn't necessarily due to the fact that they don't understand what it means to leave something or someone; what it can come down to is that they don't understand *how* it could happen.

Their Body

This is the kind of response that someone can receive if they were to say that they keep leaving their body. They could also say that they are unable to get in their body.

Another person could tell them that it is not possible for them to leave their body, as it is a part of them. Having said that, they might know what they are talking about, but if not, they might ask them to talk more about their own experience.

The Experience

However, even if someone doesn't believe that it is possible for them to leave their body, it is not going to change what is taking place. When someone leaves their body, it doesn't mean that they will actually be stepping out of it.

What it is likely to come down to is that they will disconnect from it, and this means that they won't be aware of their body. The only thing that they are likely to be aware of is what is taking place in their mind.

Looking Down

As a result of this, they won't feel as though their body is a part of them; they can actually see their body as being separate. Another way of looking at this would be to say that their attention is all in their mind.

It is then not going to be possible for them to feel grounded in their body, and they could actually feel as though they are floating. For this reason, it can be a challenge for them to feel at peace and to relax.

An Observer

When someone is in their body, it will allow them to experience life; whereas when they are in their mind, they will end up simply observing life. Therefore, when someone leaves their body, it will stop them from being able to embrace life.

So, while they will be aware of what is taking place in their mind, they won't be aware of what is taking place in their body; if they are, they might only be aware of their body's sensations. This can then mean that they will be out of touch with how they feel, and they might not know what their needs are either.

Unaware

Yet even though someone can be aware of what is happening, they could also be in a position where they are not. Thus, there will be no reason for them to talk about what is taking place in their life, as it will be the only thing they know.

At the same time, this doesn't mean that their life won't be affected by the fact they are disconnected from their body. The difference is that they won't be aware of why they are experiencing life as they are.

Common Problems

They could say that they experience a lot of anxiety and that they rarely know what they need or how they feel. They could also say that they generally feel 'ungrounded' in life, and this could cause them to engage in certain activities in order to bring them back down to earth, so to speak.

And, through being out of touch with their body, it could also mean that they are either underweight or overweight. The reason for this is that they won't know when they are hungry, and so they either won't eat when they need to, or they will eat when they don't need to.

From Time To Time

However, regardless of whether someone realises that they are disconnected from their body or not, they may have moments when they can still connect to it. On the one hand, this could be something that happens naturally, whereas on the other hand, it could happen through consciously doing something.

If it happens naturally, it could be something they experience when they are in a certain environment. When it happens through consciously doing something, it could mean that one is having a massage or doing yoga, for instance.

What's Going On?

The reason one is unable to stay in their body could be because they don't feel safe actually being in their body. So, just like one would run away to protect themselves, they leave their body to try and achieve the same outcome.

What this can mean is that they are boundaryless, and this is why they are unable to stay in their body. If they were to connect to their body, they would feel exposed, and in order to avoid feeling this way, they will simply just go into their head.

Boundaries – Are You Boundaryless?

Chapter 15

Walked Over

Do People Walk All Over You?

If someone was to lie down in a crowded place, there is a strong chance that they would end up being walked over. And it wouldn't matter if these people wanted to walk over them or not, as they wouldn't have much choice.

However, this is not to say that someone needs to do this in order to be walked over by others, as this is something that can also take place if they haven't got any boundaries. And while this can mean that other people will walk over their body, it is more likely to mean that they will be affected in other ways.

True-Self

Some people are likely to find that it is not possible for them to express their true-self, and this is because they will feel the need to go along with what other people want. It is then going to become normal for their own needs and feelings to be ignored.

On the one hand, they might be aware of what is taking place within them, but on the other hand, they could be disconnected from this part of themselves. Yet regardless of whether they are aware of what is taking place within them or not, it won't matter.

Pressure

When they are around others, they could experience an incredible amount of pressure and anxiety, and this will make it harder for them to relax. This could mean that they are focused solely on what they can do to please others.

They may also find that they end up behaving how they think other people would like them to behave, and as a result, they can lose themselves before someone else tries to take advantage of them.

Unaware

Therefore, while there are going to be people who may take advantage of them, this is not always going to be the case. Another person could come into contact with them and simply believe that their behaviour reflects who they really are.

It is then not that someone else has tried to walk over them; it is that they have simply fallen into a role. And when they fall into a role, it is likely to come down to the fact that it is what feels most safe.

A Role

When this happens, they could come across as being easy-going and only too happy to help others. Or they could come across as though they are quiet or shy, and this can then be seen as what they are like in general.

And although they may only drop into a role around certain people, it could be what they are like around everyone they meet. In the eyes of others, it is then going to be seen as who they are as opposed to a role they play in order to feel safe.

Anger

Through being walked over by others, it can be normal for them to feel angry, and this could mean that they are used to experiencing rage and even hate. The reason for this is that their anger would have built up over time, and while it could be something they experience from time to time, it could also be something that they experience on a regular basis.

Still, this doesn't mean that someone will show exactly how they feel around others, as this could be something that they only reveal when they are by themselves. But, if they don't get angry during this time, it could mean that they end up feeling depressed.

For Example

If their true feelings do come out around others, they could come out in destructive ways. There could be moments when they come across in a passive aggressive manner, or they might lose their temper for a short time.

Thus, there can be moments where they feel like a victim, and moments where they cause others to feel like a victim. And once they have settled down again, they might end up feeling guilty about this.

Career

When it comes to their career, they may work somewhere that doesn't fulfil them, and this could also be an environment where they are taken advantage of in some way. On the other hand, they may be in a position where they have been able to progress, but it is not possible for them to hold their ground.

For example, they could be a manager or have some kind of leadership position but find that they can't do their job properly. During the times when they need to act assertively, for instance, they could deteriorate.

Relationships

Along with this, they might be in a relationship where their partner takes over and doesn't allow them to be themselves. There is also the chance – which is far worse – that they are with someone who is abusive.

But if they are not in a relationship, it could be because they have had a number of relationships that were not very fulfilling. Avoiding intimacy can then be a way for them to protect themselves.

Mental Strength

If someone was to get to a place where they were no longer willing to experience life in the same way, they may end up reaching out for support. This could be a time where they hear about how they need to work on their 'mental strength'.

Through taking this approach, it will give them the ability to 'control' the feelings and thoughts that arise in them, and this will then allow them to stand up for themselves. Along with this, they might also come across information that talks about the importance of changing what they believe.

The Body

However, while there is the chance that this approach will work, there is also the chance that it won't. This is because the reason why people walk over them might be due to what is taking place in their body as opposed to their mind.

If they were to get in touch with how they feel in their body, they may find that they feel exposed. Another way of looking at this is to say that they are boundaryless, and this can then be why they don't feel comfortable standing their ground.

Chapter 16

Walls

Have You Built A Wall Around Yourself?

If someone had a garden in front of their house that they wanted to protect, it might be a good idea for them to put a fence up. This is not to say that the fence would need to go all the way along, however, as it would be important for them to have a gate put in too.

Through having a gate put in, it will not only allow them to get in and out; it will also allow other people to get in and out. The alternative would be for one to only have a fence put up, which would give them a greater level of protection, but nothing else.

Point of Focus

Someone could be in a position where the only thing they can think about is protecting their garden, and this could then stop them from thinking about having a gate put in. Based on what other people have been doing to their land, it might not be possible for them to think clearly.

And, even if someone else was to talk about how important it is for them to have a gate put in, it doesn't mean that they would necessarily listen. They could ignore or dismiss what is said, and their mind could cause them to focus on what they need to do to make sure nothing bad happens again.

Just a Fence

If they were to have a fence put in all the way around, they may believe that they have done the right thing. For instance, it won't be possible for anyone to intrude on their land, and this will stop them from having to suffer like they did before.

This could be an experience that lasts for a number of hours, and it might even go on for a number of days. However, there is likely to be a point in time when they start to suffer in another way.

Trapped

What this will come down to is that even though they have protected their garden, they have also ended up completely cutting themselves off from others. It is now no longer possible for them to see other people, let alone connect with them.

So, although they have got rid of one problem, they have ended up creating another problem in the process. They can then either carry on as they have been, or they can have part of the fence removed so they can connect with the world again.

The Sensible Option

If they were to keep things as they are, they will continue to suffer, and they may even end up losing their life. This is because they will be isolated from other people and they could soon run out of food.

Therefore, the best thing they can do is to open up their garden again through having a gate put in. However, even though this will be the sensible thing for them to do, it doesn't mean that they will actually do it.

An Example

It could be said that it is highly unlikely that one would end up fencing themselves into their own house. For one thing, they would realise what would happen and so they wouldn't allow this to take place.

However, this doesn't mean that they wouldn't fence themselves off in other ways – someone could be in a position where they keep other people at a distance, and they could do this without needing to have a physical fence around them.

Protection

Experiencing life in this way is likely to be what feels comfortable to them, and although other people may spend time with them, it will be a challenge for them to get close to them. Thus, even though they spend time with others, they may as well be by themselves.

As a result of this, it might not matter how much they suffer, as it is not going to be possible for them to let anyone in. Other people could see them as being guarded, and they might wonder why they are this way.

Out of Touch

Having said that, they could generally be out of touch with their need to connect with others, and this will then mean that, for now, it won't be a problem. During these moments, they will be comfortable with how their life is.

But when they do have moments when they are aware of their need to connect with others, they could end up feeling angry and powerless. This could then be a sign that they are not aware of why they can't connect with others and embrace life.

Two Experiences

If someone experiences life in this way, it will be normal for them to feel as though they have no control over their life. And until they realise why they are experiencing life in this way, their outlook is unlikely to change.

On the other hand, if someone is aware of the fact that they only feel comfortable when they keep people at a distance, they might not feel so powerless. This is because they will realise that it's not about other people; it's about what is going on for them.

Opening Up

When someone is able to open up, their life can become far more fulfilling, and this is why it can be hard for someone to understand why they would build walls around themselves in the first place. However, in order for them to open up, they will need to feel as though it is safe for them to do so.

The reason they don't feel safe enough to open up is likely to be because they are boundaryless. As they don't feel as though they can protect themselves around others, they have no other choice than to keep other people at a distance.

Chapter 17

Weight

Are You Overweight?

If someone is in a position where they are not as slim as they would like to be, it is not going to be hard for them to find other people who are having the same experience; this is because it is something that a lot of people struggle with.

The Media

For one thing, the mainstream media often talks about certain celebrities who are unable to keep their weight down, with there being times when they have their ideal weight and times when they don't.

Along with this, they also focus on the ones who were once slim and who ended up gaining a lot of weight. And, even when they are not talking about celebrities, they talk about how this is something that affects normal people.

Not Alone

Thus, someone only needs to read a paper or a magazine, for instance, to see that they are not the only ones in this position. Having said that, they might not even need to go this far, and this is due to the fact that they may know a few people personally who also have the same problem.

When they are around these people, they can often talk openly about how frustrating it is to carry more weight than they need to carry. In fact, they could feel as though they can relax when they are around these kinds of people.

One Step Further

There is also the chance that most of their friends are in the same position, and this can then show that it's because they feel comfortable with them. They may find that they can be themselves around them, and that they don't need to put on any kind of act.

And while they may give each other the support they need when it comes to losing weight, this might not actually be the case. Instead, they could come to believe that there is nothing wrong with their weight.

Two Sides

Therefore, when someone is around people who have the same problem as them, it could end up having a positive effect on their life; the support they receive can make it easier for them to lose weight.

However, if someone comes to believe that there is nothing wrong with their weight, it could cause them to go against their true needs. Of course, with all the time they spend around these people, it might not be possible for them to actually realise this.

Health

Along with this, it could also set them up to have health problems; however, this is something that can all depend on how much excess weight they are carrying. For example, there is naturally going to be a difference between carrying a few extra pounds and carrying a few extra hundred pounds.

The General Approach

If someone wanted to lose weight, there is a strong chance that they would end up going on some kind of diet. And this could be something that has taken place on a number of occasions.

If someone spends most of their life on a diet, they may have a certain diet that they go on, or they might have been on a number of different ones. Through doing this, they may find that even though they lose weight when they are on the diet, they soon gain it again when they come off.

Round in Circles

There can then be moments in their life when they have their ideal weight, and moments when they don't. As a result of this, they could wonder if it is really worth all the effort, and during these moments, they could feel hopeless.

This could then mean that they end up eating more than they need to (or eating the wrong kinds of food), gaining a few more pounds in the process. They can then feel even worse about themselves, and this can cause them to eat too much again, with this whole process continuing to play out.

Acceptance

But if one was in a position where they were overweight, and this was something that caused part of them to feel uncomfortable, it doesn't mean that they will necessarily do anything about it. They could find that another part of them feels comfortable this way.

And this part could be a lot stronger than the part of them that wants them to lose weight. This is not to say that they are going to be aware of these two parts, but it is something that will control their life nevertheless.

Protection

There are a number of reasons why someone would be in a position where they are unable to keep their weight down and/or feel comfortable being overweight, and one of the reasons why they could be this way is because it is a way for them to protect themselves. So, when this weight is not on their body, they will end up feeling exposed.

Thus, it won't matter how it makes them look or the effect it has on their self-esteem and health, as their own survival is going to take precedence. Another way of looking at this would be to say that one is boundaryless, and their body is using what it can in order to protect them from harm.

Boundaries – Are You Boundaryless?

Chapter 18

Developing Boundaries

Whether you can relate to just some of these challenges (or all of them) as well as others, there is a strong chance that you just want to move forward with your life. Perhaps you have only just realised that you haven't developed any boundaries, or you may have been working on this area for quite some time.

However, no matter what has taken place so far, the main thing is that you have kept moving forward. At times, it is not always possible to take the direct route in life, and this can cause us to believe that we are going off course.

Persistence

However, as long we can keep going and don't give up, I believe that we will get to where we need to be, or achieve what we need to achieve. This is why it is important to be able to take action, to have the ability to tolerate frustration, and to trust in the process of life.

If you have been trying to develop boundaries for a while, you may have experienced a lot of frustration. This can include the pain you have felt through not having boundaries, as well as the pain that you've experienced through trying things that haven't worked.

Awareness

On the other hand, if you have only just realised that you haven't got any boundaries, there may only be the pain you have experienced as a result of being wide open. This is not to say that you have experienced either more or less pain that someone else; what it comes down to is that there can be a difference.

The most important thing is that you are aware of how your life is being affected through being in a boundaryless state. As you may now know, without this understanding it is easy to get caught up in the symptoms.

Two Options

If you have spent time doing this, it may mean that you've focused on what is taking place in your head or that you've changed your own behaviour. This may have been something that has had an effect on you for a short while, or it might not have done anything.

The mind is often seen as the most important area when it comes to experiencing life differently, and while the mind can't be overlooked, it doesn't mean that there isn't more to it. Just as our behaviour is also important, but once again, it can be given more attention than is necessary.

Exposed

At one point in time, focusing on your mind and your behaviour might have seemed like the right approach to take. For instance, this could be because an expert recommended it to you, or you may have read about it in a book.

But, as time has passed (and you may have always sensed this), you have come to see that this approach doesn't always work. It may also occur to you that as you feel exposed and don't feel safe in your own body, it is not going to be enough for you to change your thoughts and to act differently.

The Body

Ultimately, the area that needs most of your attention is your body, and this is an area that is often overlooked in today's world. As, although what is taking place in our mind can influence how we feel and how we behave, what is taking place in our body can also play a part in how we feel and what we do.

It is here that we can carry trapped emotions and trauma. If you are carrying trapped emotions in your body, for instance, it is highly unlikely that you will be able to remove them by thinking differently or changing your behaviour.

Emotional Pain

This can be the pain that you've experienced through not getting your needs met at an early age. As, if these needs were met, there is a strong chance that you would have developed boundaries.

This pain can include the loss that you experienced, anger, rage, powerlessness, hopelessness, helplessness, guilt, and shame. It will be important for you to process this emotional build-up, and this can take place through using SHEN therapy or another method for processing emotions.

Two Parts

Finding the right technique is one thing, but another important part of this is finding a therapist that you feel comfortable with; when you find someone you feel comfortable with, it will be a lot easier for you to move forward.

However, at the same time, if you find that you can't relax, it doesn't necessarily mean that you are working with the wrong person. What it could mean is that it might take you a while to settle down.

Trauma

You may find that as you process the emotional pain that is within you, you can gradually begin to feel safe in your own body. However, there is also the chance that this will only get you so far.

The next step will then be for you to deal with the trauma that is actually trapped in your body. In order to do this, you can experience some kind of body work.

Hypnotherapy

Hypnotherapy is also something that can deal with the trauma within you. Through getting in touch with the moments where you experienced trauma, you will be able to change the memories, and this can stop them from having a negative effect on your life.

Passed Down

There is also the chance that the trauma within you didn't start with you, and that it has in fact been passed down. Therefore, if you were abused and/or neglected, this could have been an experience that a number of your ancestors went through.

In this case, you can heal yourself through giving back what doesn't belong to you, and this is something that can take place through having a family constellation.

Two Sides

On the one hand, this will allow you to heal the trauma that you have been carrying around for all this time, and on the other hand, it will allow you to give back to your family what doesn't belong to you; what can affect our ability to have boundaries and a strong sense of self is when we are still enmeshed to our family.

So, once these two things have taken place, it will be possible for you to be yourself.

This is something that can take place in a workshop or through having a one-to-one session, though there is also the chance that you will need to have more than one constellation.

Support

Having the right support around you during this time is always important. As you begin to change, you may find that you are no longer drawn to some people, and that other people will start coming into your life.

Another important element will be for you to make sure you eat properly and get the exercise you need during this time – this will give you the energy you need to keep going.

Final Thoughts

Like most things in life, this is a process and not something that will happen overnight. So, when you can see that you are moving forward, make sure you acknowledge what has taken place. When this isn't the case, do what you can to be compassionate towards yourself.

After all, this is a journey and it takes courage to do this kind of work; if it was easy, everyone would be doing it.

Boundaries – Are You Boundaryless?

Acknowledgements

Over the past few years, there have been a number of people who have been there for me and who have shown their support. This has been a time when I have been working on my own boundaries.

Vijay Rana is someone who has made a big difference in my life. If it wasn't for his support, my life would have been a lot harder.

There has also been the continued support of Sheila Banyham, and it was through her that I was able to meet Ian Baillie.

It has been a real blessing to have met him, and he has been a very supportive figure ever since the day we met, so thank you for being there for me.

Fairly recently I met someone called Wain Gordan, and he seemed to come out of nowhere. I met him during a time when I was helping a friend move house.

This is someone who has a mind like a samurai sword; he is extremely sharp and on the ball. It has been an honour to get to know him and to exchange ideas with each other.

Printed in Great Britain
by Amazon